SHADOW PARADISE

ISBN: 978-0-6455211-0-8

Printed and bound in Australia by Lightning Source

In dedication to forgiveness, in the darkest of times

Of self

God Bless and love.

For what is paradise?

If one not knows the shadows

··CONTENTS··

PART II

DANCING WITH DEATH

PART III

REBIRTH

PART IV

REFUGE

SHADOW PARADISE

••○••

INTRODUCTION

From the dawn of late teens
Time exists on the screens
In isolated confinement
And out of divine alignment

For a decade…

Separation, it has caused
And time paused
Stolen hours on the round face
In its darkest embrace.

'At sixteen, I was taken to the table where they incised humans. A lens was inserted, travelling down my vocal tunnel. When I woke, I hadn't come back the same... The fluid that sent me into a deep buzz, stole my soul; ruptured and shattered me to pieces.

"How do I find my way back to me?"

Akin to a cracked mirror of a thousand pieces, lost in space and time. Not knowing how to bind the pieces back together and where some of them had gone.'

•••

Enter:
Be careful when you do,
Make sure to follow my lead
And watch my footsteps too,
So you can make it out alive
And not get lost
(Or even death-dive)
Into the ice and frost
Frozen.

PART I

THE FOG

••○••

Binding a mother
To her daughter
Is the cord at birth
Cut here, on Earth

DEAR MUM

My dear mum:
I need you

I am crying
Please respond

I'm in danger,
I cannot feel my legs

I cannot respond
I'm off the ground

And all you'd need to say
Is 'everything will be okay'

(The cord cut.)

Like a broken record
Of this sad discord
The same chapter on repeat
And everyone is defeat
Unless one reads
The hidden deeds

History Repeats

A dark aura fills me with angst.
Take me to a trench
Or the terrain of a nightmare,
It can't compare to this darkness –

Gestecke's blossom, grass grows,
But I do not, not my mind –

In the midst of the battlefield
Fate is in the hands of the enemy,
The web of my wired brain
Mapping out roots of mighty pain;
Sieves drain mental sanity,
Separating reality from delusion
Its wires capture me,
Imprison me within cognitive fog.

A gulag landscapes my vision
Of enslavement to the beast.

EARLY LIFE

Many people are here:
There is a rise in tension,
In the way I show and appear
To the increased, apprehension

Seconds are hours and days are weeks;
There is no end to this torment.
A rise in blood and redness in cheeks
Shows my fear, dormant

No one notices.
Going by missed
With the disruptive choices
That are dismissed.

MY MONSTER

My monster lays awake at night,
My heart rattles in its thoracic cage,
Seconds turn to minutes and minutes turn to hours
Running along that hellish stage –

Through me, like a runners' sense of
Being – shaking, sweating, pounding –
Adrenaline infiltrates. Prim and proper,
Does not describe me.

Hours of thought tame and quiet,
Drawing the monster into its closure
Where it can never hurt me, but be kind –

Time will only tell when he will be gone,
For hands clasped in prayer, hope.

Anxiety, awakens senses:
A survival response
To keep one safe
From external threats

When tormented in sleep
The true threat is oneself
And the mind
Of which it endlessly wonders

CONFLICT

We are like soldiers in a battle.
Against the enemy we stand
In defiance, fighting for our right
In life, to feel freedom -

From being trapped
In a tornado of prescriptions
We both break free together,
One influencing the other.

We are fresh, raw and tender
Our minds, both full of ideas
Wanting desperately to unite –
A connection so strong
As the linked arms of comrades

A beautiful day mirrors this flight
Out of hell into holy waters
Where we take a stride into
The sways and swirls of utopia.

No one will ever find me here
To be flattened and saddened
Like pre-opened pillboxes
That steal poetic innocence

Unable to fight and write
Against my medicated mind;
Dancing on cold and hot water,
A lost and confused author.

SPLITTING

Happy and sad
I am joyful and mad.

Lots of company but none.
I am not finished but done.

I didn't drink, but I'm drunk,
Floating once and then sunk.

I am open but closed in –
Faithless, singing this hymn

Lost within this riddle
Feeling all so little.

A fine line exists
Between the exits
And heart beats –
So fine it will tear
If one is dare
To touch the twine.

DEATH'S DANCE

Awakened by the wilt of warmth,
  Running 'round to find refuge

Hearing that thump of heartbeats
  Tuning to that tick-tock talk –

Jitter jumps scream jargon noise
As white knuckles show new nerves

And, scrambling through my stash
  Popping that plastic sealer

To at last, find long relief
To this sense of ghastly grief.

Never quite fit in
Anywhere I'm soarin'
In this reality
Of polar duality

INVERTED PLANE

This world wasn't made for the queer
In its perfectly orchestrated sphere.

Compassion and emotion aren't priority
As this doesn't suit the majority.

My problems differ from the normal
(They're considered abnormal).

Hearing sounds that aren't there,
A feeling so uncommon and rare,

I escape being mentally inundated
While society lines up to be medicated –

As they self-medicate to induce
Colourful chemicals, in their brain juice,

Unknowing as to what it'll bring
Except a cloud of misery and suffering.

MY WORLD

Twirling around in my world
As soon as I stopped I hurled

At the disgust
Of the strong trust
One has in authority
And all that governs she and he.

Watching the sun rise
I sit there and despise
The way things have ended up,
How coffee sits solemnly in a cup

All calm in pure forms
But once drunk, transforms
Into stimulation
And brain activation.

This duplicate image
Exhibits the damage
That left me a shaking mess

On this damned shipwreck
All a trick, so sick

Dwelling on the past
Shows me the contrast
Of how things were
Leaving me to comply
To a life of no win
In this fucking trash bin.

Val – Ee – Yum is so yum
It hits the eardrum –
In a place that hums
Me to sleep,
So deep

TRANQUILIZER MIRAGE

That hypnotic sensation of becoming unwound
Exists within the chemicals that bind
Emotions fading within the mind
Until they disintegrate causing me to grind.

Scrawls of a lifetime supply
Of high peaks, deliriums and euphoria
Lead me nothing, but to comply
To a stiffness of solid composure.

Equilibrium is at poise when high
Opening the two-hour window of glory
Following are two days of clouded sky
Above this illusory panacean story.

A fantasy, illusion and dream
Furnish this house of hell,
Of all that fits within this profitable stream
By the dollar bills from Clientele.

Sedating substances
Reduce the incidences
Of memoirs from the past
So vast
Of trauma and pain
A collection or perhaps domain –
On encore
I feel at war

STOLEN INNOCENCE

Where is my sensational swing?
I can no longer see and jump,
Its strength has truncated
And severity abbreviated.

Could have these chemicals diminished
My real and unhinged demeanour
Of fun, energetic and magnifique lifestyle
Full of glitter, confetti and sparkle?

I want to hear and see
All the imaginary and incredible,
Where my mind can take me
On a beautiful odyssey.

Now absent, this colourful soul,
I no longer distinguish the real me,
As I will just be
A medically mended version of me.

OBSESSION

A character called Mary Jane
Elegantly pirouettes through my brain
To a twenty-four by seven chain,
To the high tunes, eliminating pain.

Diversions are what put me by bay
To her gracefulness and beauty
Crashing onto the nugget of feathers, I lay,
Twirling into a frenzy, for her line of duty.

Hands clasped and kneeled down
Under the twinkling light of the stars:
It's how these devious figures drown –
Freedom from behind iron bars,

Strapped and leashed by them
Substituting high for subjection,
Power now propelling them,
Me, enhancing their remuneration.

Solicitude is in complete absence,
White gowns are used as scapegoats
All that I feel and sense
Is desperation for green notes.

Inner voice gives reason to action
Especially when there is movement
In the direction
Toward the destination

POETIC VOICE

I miss his voice
When will he come back?

He was a friend to me.
No feelings of being alone…

Murmurs and mumbles
Microphones and ensembles

Backing me into the corner,
Waiting, for the moment to slaughter
Me.

My actions fail to control.
He's taken over my soul.

Ridding his presence, I stop
All that I am doing and drop

My paper and pen down
And sit there like a clown:

Down trickle invisible tears
Craving his voice in my ears.

Without the voice: lost
With the voice, it cost
And taxed my sanity
And questioned my reality.

For I am whole with voice,
But fragmented without.

In his office, again I am here
To get my next fix
As he begins to mix
My next round of wild ride
As my dad patiently waits outside
Rolling his eyes
Knowing the lies

ANOTHER DOSE

Suppressed my ability to write
In tune, with poetic sight,
To put black ink onto scroll,
Like that of a newspaper.

It's stolen my strand of rhyme
During this medicated time,
Unable to put word to word
As all reads out, absurd.

Every verse feels struggled
As it all sounds so jumbled
With no logical flow,
In this depressing shallow.

It's taken me a while
To write something worthwhile,
Something that sounds good,
About my story in adulthood.

Living in the mind
A prison in disguise
Keeping you confined
To all the lies
That fuel existence
In extreme resistance

THOUGHTS

Round and round in circles they go
Till they make the anger grow.
They tease the mind
And aren't so kind
They trick the brain
Making one go insane
And thinking something is true
But one doesn't have a clue
Whether it's real
Or just a dodgy deal.

It will never be clear
As to what one hears
It may be logical, or instead;
Crazy and diabolical

Wishing for once
To jump on them and pounce
Down on those thoughts
That play ping-pong on tennis courts
That don't follow rules

But end up winning jewels
Of the mind –

It fucks with the head
Can't ever get ahead,
Shivers and then goose bumps
Taking the mind to the dumps
Where one stands in silence
All stiff and densely tense.

Connections are destroyed
Of every synapse
Of the brain; collapse.
As one feels deployed
From reasoning properly
And thoughts, arranged accordingly.

On and off
Back and forth
Pills kept me safe
From trauma

WITHDRAWING

So cold, so alone.
In this dark tone
They all try and assist
As I try and persist
Through these last steps
In these dark depths
Of cold ocean water
As I prepare to slaughter
The last of my treatment
Of this pill assortment.

They refuse to support
The last of my journey
Out of these wicked haystacks
Full of pins and thumbtacks
Stabbing my body in all ways
As the sun beams down its rays.

My choice to come clean
Disrupts their habitual routine.

The person I used to trust,
But now clearly distrust, disagrees.
He is part of the foundation
Of this medicated nation.

His curvy, upside-down smile
Makes my mind run a mile
Around the real intentions
Causing my facial tensions.

Fear and paranoia fill me
And my cup of tea
With threads of doubt
Sewn to my wired tapestry,
Questioning his purpose
And all he stands for.

ONCE AGAIN

Once again
I fall into their trap,
Into this sticky sap
Where I'm immobile,
In this pill pile
Where this quicksand
Makes it hard to stand,
Melting into the land
I grip with my hand,
Against the force
Through this hard course,
Of this medication
In slow repetition,
Down the vortex
Where I hit the apex –
Yet, I must endure
To become fully cured,
Another harsh withdrawal
Where I will crawl
To get to the place
Prior to this race

Where life was polychromatic
And happiness ecstatic.

One will search for me
Once they've hit rock bottom.
Often they disagree with what I present
But if they follow they will blossom
I offer solutions that work
Getting them out of anguish –
Of ache, suffering and electric jerks
And heal all ailments, to vanish –
Truth.

THE PATH OF FREEDOM

Battering like a beastly blitz, a foreign world
Of square chairs and banana shaped pears
Unknown to this inverted world
Of the diverted and converted.
Medicinal liquids induce spirals
Of untrustworthy trials
And misdiagnosis of all those under hypnosis.
There are many of us,
But we are ones against thousands.
Of all the rounds of professionals we see
A pop of a pill means they drill
Into the minds of us.
The minds they don't trust.
A walk outside, is out of sight
Our freedom is stripped
And violently ripped, teased and tugged
Under that grey rock rug.
A bed, a stream, a plant is all that's there –
In our room, where we are left.
"We will be let out,' is all we hear
Coming in through our ear.
False hopes fulfil our thoughts

Letting us become distraught.
We wake up with hope, praying that
We might cope with what the day will bring
And what song we will sing.
It will only take one mistake to bring us down,
With what makes us drown in this miserable place
That I call our space, in the dark and black ocean
Where I take my saviour potion.
Sad and hopeless is standard.
It's all that we get granted
As we deserve nothing more
Because we are drawn and torn, like stick figures
Hit by triggers, buckled and bolted in the middle
Making them look little.

It's time we took a stance
Showed them our dance
Hold our hands
Releasing those tight bands
Everyone gets out
Just stand up and shout
The walkways in sight

A path or perhaps a fight
Is all it will take
For our freedom's sake
Out of this wicked mess
That's caused all stress.

Freedom resides within:
Externally seeking it
Further validates
One is not free

Like a shadow
To seek light
Because it is not light
But darkness

For the light
Will not seek light
As it is the light –
Be the light

Isolation disconnects.
Unity connects.

Sweet Flame

Claps and applauds illude my perceptions.
Smiles and laughter foreshadow my vision.
I am not alone tonight.
(I am with an orchestra of souls.)

Twenty-one alight the night;
On top of a layer of sweet lump
That crown glistens on my head
In a way it never did before.

An array of pops to the head
Should have killed me before
Perseverance and strength prevailed
To be able to see the rays today.

•••

PART II

DANCING WITH DEATH

••○••

DESTROYED

Feeling so alone
While I sing in this tone:
How'd I get here?

A thought to disappear
With no motion of voice –
It's left me no choice
But to think of termination
As I've got no determination
To remain on Earth
Stuck under the red turf
With tied up and knotted roots
And rotted green shoots
As my soundless yell
Comes out, from under hell.

My addiction to anything
Within this boxing ring,
With only myself
Destroying my health –
It's not what I want
But a pill,

Is on my will and
No one comprehends
When showing my truth
Caught red-handed
All alone and stranded.

It is simple to be told
Or given a hand to hold
When feeling sunken
(Or the brain on malfunction)
But all this assistance
Makes no difference
To this melancholy
In this empty body

NOT LONG NOW

Expiration is creeping up on me
Sensing the feelings of he

Who whispers and conjures
In my head and injures

My frame of thought, to continue
On this road, so rocky.

At this time no one knows,
All that is left goes

Drafting out my plan
Of what to plan –

What will be the easiest way
To leave and go far away –

To a peaceful place
Where I won't pace –

Up and down hallways
Driving myself into doorways.

Stabbing the heart of those
Who are around me and dispose of

The actions I wish to carry out
In order to finally escape

All this craziness
In this haziness

Finding the right time
To commit this crime –

Like lottery numbers
It leaves me in wonders

Of either…

A dip in the pool
Means I need no tool;

An intake of circular powder
Might make the thoughts scream louder;

A leap onto two iron lines
Is like stepping onto landmines.

Instead of crushed and dead
Paralysed in bed.

For what is deemed logic
When all possibilities sound tragic?

First comes the depression
Next is the progression
Of contemplation
In desperation
Of a situation
Of demolition
And then comes the letter…

THE LETTER

To self:

I know you may be feeling down,
Feeling like you want to drown
Yourself in deep, cold water,
Slit your throat and slaughter
Your life away to the dead.

This feeling will surely pass soon,
Just wait at least till noon and
Don't give in to the thoughts
Tying you up in knots
And doling out depression in lots.

I know you want to overdose,
To take the pills and
Then sit down, chill –
To drift into a sleep
Deceased, with no peep.

Or to drive off to the near rocks,
To jump off and drop down

Into the depths of dark blue,
Into a bloody stew
Of splattered grey bones.

This phase takes over your thoughts,
Left to think you're distraught
It robs you
Of presence,
Making you stagnant
And a strong magnet
Of discomfort.

If thought of death claims victory,
It tampers logic, so slippery.
Don't let your guard down low
Where seeds are sewn below,
Where you can't see
For what will be.

From yours truly,
Death

Melting into self
Collapsing on the couch.
Losing sense of the clock
And all surroundings

As I approach God

AFTERLIFE

Tantamount to those pearly gates,
A step up provides closer views
Of the angelic world that awaits
In different shades and vibrant hues.

Senses return to their full effect,
Cuisines are tasteful in many ways
As I am now able to fully detect
The missed favourites on previous days.

Now, long awaiting a good ol' drink
Of bitter vodka and lemon lime,
Clashing glasses and hearing the clink
Makes every sip count for lost time.

The dark world left behind
Will never be consigned to oblivion.
As what remains within the mind
Are ashes of pain and burns of addiction.

From the heart of hell
To the heights of heaven

I am now free from the dependency spell.
In a total of seven gruelling months.

Limbo is non-existent in this instance:
It is an all high or an all low
Where I must correctly balance a stance
For full effect of positive flow.

For now, the inferno is long lost –
Calamity will not prevail –
As I make no plans to return to the host
Of the catastrophic events entailed.

•••

PART III

REBIRTH

••○••

It was destiny that I returned
After all I had learnt
To come clean
And to see green
Much brighter than before –
And sounds heard more raw
The surroundings more active:
Birthing existence, so reactive.

COLOUR

We sit, we hit
That throttle
Of that pill bottle
Left behind
In the time of rewind.
Now un-medicated
I'm able to lose that weight
Of poisonous pleasure
That's of large measure.
A digital age
Opens up this new page.
Of fast flying wheeled boxes
Jumping over running foxes;
A delusive power of reason
Puts me in a frenzied season
Of lighted squares
While I sit on airborne chairs
Feeling that rush
Of the digital paintbrush
Painting that large complex
Of vibrant and colourful sex.
Breathless and amazed, it

Leaves me vividly dazed,
Craving for more
On that dance floor.

A PARALLEL OCCURRENCE

In a world non-native
He isn't human anymore:
They give him a regulative
To control his core.

A story so sincere
Sitting there in silence
I listen to the story of dear he
As authorities protest in defiance.

His heart skips two beats
Then processes one, two and three
Sitting rigidly on the seats
Like a lumbar under a bean tree

His delivery of quarrel
Is a copy of my record
Of a tale that sounds immoral
When written on their clipboard.

All he needed was an angels' hand
To give him the touch of relief

Drawing him back to common land
Where you and I
Have faith in his belief.

The detrimental impacts of what is advocated
Is not acknowledged by those who advocate it
But
Only those who receive the advocate
Can be understood by those who received it –
A secret language.

PART III

UNWANTED PART

Shackled chains
Showing unwanted stains
Helping him claim
His renowned fame.

His time has expired
As he sits there tired
Reminiscing on life
In agonizing strife.

His presence sent me in fury
His smile and frown curvy
I couldn't foresee
For what would come to be…
His sounds had no logic
His actions were beyond tragic
That single glance
In silence…
Showed me now, he wanted to dance.

So slippery and cunning
Now, my vision slightly hazy

For when he would infiltrate
Thinking, he was so great.

I could have had him
But I didn't want to raise hell
So I let out a brief comment
Secretly questioning his assortment
Of where he belongs
In the old folks' songs
Within my records.

TORN WITHIN

"I am here now
With a smile and a frown"
That's what they'll all say
But I can't seem to display
That crooked tilt
Inducing false guilt.
It's all too exciting
And inside of me, I'm fighting
Those demons that remain
That are on ventures
In the hidden corners
Of which I can't complain
To anyone because
They'll laugh and take the piss.

I'm in a land so peaceful
But still so full
Of shaking thoughts
Attached to mental cords
Tying me down
From harmonious sounds
Of beautiful birds
That chirp and chirp
As I am hurt.

THE TRUTH

Hurry hurry!
In need of a miracle
Running round in a circle
Thought after thought
Bending now and all taut.

I continuously try and try
Keep telling myself I'd die
To keep moving forward
Heading so steadily, toward-
"The LORD"

There at least I have hope
Where I'm able to cope
Through this devastation
Causing me agitation.

At midpoint of the dipole,
Split apart, is my soul
Stuffing up my life
And cutting, with a knife

I never cut, but I do get cut
When others diss me and shut
The door in my path
And cut down low at the calf.

Contrary to a fairy-tale
It's caused a face, so pale

Like when others see a ghost
But I can call him my host

Of misery and constant pain
That comes in droplets of rain
Like a sprinkle of water
From the eye of your daughter.

When you catch her
She tries to slaughter –
Try to deal with that
Then you'll count on the stat
Debating submission or war;
It's a pain making me feel torn
Between two worlds
Of straightness and curls

Indecisiveness: clueless and shoeless
I'm becoming less and less
With the choices so hostile
Closer comes, that pill pile.

Buckling to the floor like a bitch
As I constantly struggle and twitch
Looking up, wishing at every flying star…
This is the true story by far.

POWER OF TIME

A long era of patiently waiting
For when it will end –
This pain.

Exertion of flutter and scatter
Spirals into a walk of wonder,

Lost in the leaden forest
Of all I can recall
Materialised by white petals
And orange gems
They call them
Chamomile, passionflower
A gift,
Healing me and the collywobbles.

A stammered pace drives to the sea
To the ear, the sound of ocean breeze
Fades away the buzzing whir and
Quiver of bugs under the skin.

The etiolated pasture, now green,
That dried up creek now flows a stream.

An extinct creature, a rising new
A fractured perception: all healed.

Father time screams "ding dong dang"
As the hands move making a clang

Karma: time.
Take two
And two will be taken from you

WINDOWS

That slow and sluggish pace
Holds tearful feelings in embrace
Through the scenery of green,
Allowing me to start clean.

The cool breeze through my hair
Entwines those worries of despair
Into fine and pristine plaits
That get tied and tossed into hats.

Strong gusts empower me
To at last feel free and
With each stride of pride
I feel no need to hide.

They call them windows and waves
When you're in the darkest of caves
Of electric and shock-like days
In the thick and foggiest haze

MY CRAZY

His venom enters me
Infiltrating my red fluid
So rapidly
Nourishing me with life.
Dancing on tables
Kicking down empty seats
Twirling to the tunes he sings to me.

A buzz or thrill
Is what he gives me and
Leaping out to the stars
I touch them with grace
Then fall back into his nest
With comfort and certainty.

FIRST LOVE

Like the birth of a dove
New to the world
All tight and curled
My first steps are a guess
Of where to go next
A paddle down the stream
Under that glistening sunbeam
Leads me to halfway point,
Where I risk being at gunpoint.
Now, the transpose of goods
With whom, comes from the woods.
I give a bag of dollar
For the workings of gold collar.

Grateful for my mother's gift
I reach into my pocket and lift
For that rumpled and dried-up docket
Trapped and sealed in a plastic socket.

It was my first kiss:
A strange and peculiar bliss

Ambushed within a daydream
By powerful and mystical steam

Paralysed by the holy fern, that
Hypnotised me in the sweat, bitter cold
And kept me all composed.

Living alone on this Earth
Without growing from the turf
Punctures my heart from within
Caving itself in.

113

HEIGHTENED SENSES

He calls my name
I feel the fame
Of him calling me
But I cannot see
Anyone calling
It's appalling.
Waves of voice
Given a choice
Pound through microphones
In all types of tones.
Confusing my mind
Trying to find
That man
Who ran
My thoughts
Who system rorts
Stealing my moments
And all my saviour tents –
Pegged into the ground
Destroyed by sound
He blurs my auditory tunnel

Adding a huge funnel
To that cove of arched skin
With a straight metal pin.
And looking like a fool
I stand drenched in drool
Immersed now in a daydream pool
Of distortion
Out of proportion
Floating in air
A feeling so rare.

CHARACTER: THE WITCH

She said "I was cackling"
Like a hysterical witch
On fire in the haystacks
Tied down (nowhere to run)
Demonized and berserk
Her four-legged creature
Was even startled by her –
Her presence reflected fear
Off the googly goggles of her close tribe
Her behaviour was unorthodox.

Racing to her beloved
For even he, unfamiliar
With her bizarre disposition:
She called out, 'Proctor!'
He turned, unknowing.

Showing no alliance
Hysterical and demented
Crazed and unhinged
Illustrates the picture of her.

MILLION DOLLAR DREAM

A backyard of trees and delicate shrubbery
A six-point leaf in plentiful amounts
Emerald, lime, sage and olive
A thrill rolls up as I count
A secrecy to keep this from getting out

Dream, a million dollar bill
Could this all be truly real?

Stems growing from large pots of water
Are the best of their kind
(Beaming sparks of energy promotes growth)

Slowly, the plants are taken astray
My fortune beings to slowly slip away –
And I awake.

The money remains in dreams
It can't cross the realms
The dream plane has no similarity
To Earth heavy in density
So heavily dense you'll be rich.

THE TOLL ON THE SOUL

Running in circles around the face
Of that clock, driving me insane;
Up and down, I constantly pace
Looking to the sun, through that pane.

Burnt out, ashy circles
Hoop those black pupils,
So common, like rehearsals
And alike; quadruples'.

A drag race of two stories
In my speedy paced head
Conflicting for their territories
Until one is burned and falls dead

An influx of magnificent ideas
Fortunes and luck engulf me
A foreign feeling – idiosyncrasy –
An extremity so carefree.

That blood most similar
Is now the most unfamiliar;

My face is foreign in the mirror
And so to the universe, is my aura.

Entering this state
Begins to infiltrate me
Creating a hole in my fuel tank
Stealing from my energy bank.

THE CONQUERED

I didn't finish the race.
I fell short of a heartbeat
But to avoid defeat
He said I attained freedom

He was all solid concrete,
Blood, redness and heat
No emotion
And no devotion.

Every move was a forced vibration
To get him to his destination:
Pride, ego and machismo
Is what left me laughing sarcastically.

Awed and admiring my purity
Expectations to uphold my dignity
Striving for mass cultivation
Left him standing in isolation.

My work here is done
I won the race
In my heart
I conquered
This deliberating disgrace.

MYSTIC

Diamonds, glitter, glitz and glam
Sparkles shine from beneath the dam.

Flying with wings spanned wide
Tears of joy have never lied

About far and long journeys
Unlocked by clear-cut keys

Opening up a new dimension
Of existence, of ascension

That grips my mind
Under this long bind

Of a frizzy thought that spirals
Into mystical fairy tale vials

Stored within my pumping core.

Under the floating green palm
Laying on blue crystal, all calm

Tossing away that box of time
I form another invention of rhyme

Taking me to places,
Occupying peaceful spaces

In the clouds-sky high –
Sending down the watered cry,

Mystified and magical moments
Save me from all harsh elements

That live in my mind, a fracture
From tyrants that puncture –

A deep and circular hole
Filled up with burnt, black coal.

And finally, leaving the underworld,
Now standing on a new world,

In a world where I belong
Comfortably singing this song.

•••

PART IV

REFUGE

••○••

THE TREE OF LIGHT

Standing alone on a hill of emerald
Rooted into the *terra firma*
Swaying to the pulsating waves of wind
Like a perfect dancer to tunes
Of vibrating sound waves and beats
Progressing a few strides towards

Landing under its arm of destiny
I glance upwards and observe
Sunbeams filling the open gaps.
I take my first leap up
Grabbing onto a web of branches
That she gives saving me from the fall
Venturing for the beams of light energy
Giving this spirit a way of life.

A rugged climb further upward
Gives way to an inch of flood
A tear drop
As it falls: it lands and hydrates
The roots' thirst

Another look up into the peaks of light and
I persevere and proceed climbing.

As nights and days go by
I nest myself into a bird-built home.
Resisting the elements as they occur.
I persevere and continue
This journey of life.

Near the top, excitement fills me with
A pounding pump of adrenaline, which
Enters and exits my red fluid tunnels
Giving me my last strife of fuel;
I push through and see the landscape
Of grey mist in the night violence,
Electrical shocks and loud claps,
A storm so severe
Then, to disappear.

This tree; my light.

Refuge is found when
Sharing indistinguishable emotions
With common people
In similar circumstances

TRUE FRIEND

We have finally united
A lifelong friendship
Longing to meet
Dine together and greet
One another –
And each other.
We share common ground
Of a mentally loud sound
That drove us crazy
Yet turned us to a daisy.

Like a mirror reflection
Akin in complete perfection.
Our experiences overlap
Like a felt collage
Perfectly on a mirage.
The best of friend
That I had befriended –
For without her
Brain waves couldn't deter
All the colossal damage
That added years to my age.

She picks me up through
Thick and sticky, brain dew
Despite the rain, hail, shine
Or when, in motion of decline.

She says:
"Stretch your heart and extend
It's walls of capacity
To me, your best friend
When dark thought is your centre,
And I will be your mentor."

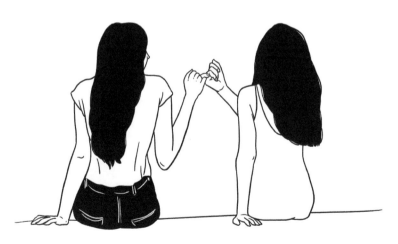

PENELOPE

You are the symbols on my staff lines
You give me nothing but hope
When I waddle and crawl over landmines
On this fine and skinny tightrope

I am the cause of my distress
In all of this intense mess
But your attendance and presence
Pulls me back into a state of transcendence.

You give me endless energy,
Singing the highest of all dotted notes
That I can recall in my memory,
About all past anecdotes.

You are to visit me more often
Because when you do
You make my destructive days shorten
And all that bothers me too.

Your presence comes at an expense:
You pull and tug my guitar strings

Causing them to come out and dispense
Like the zings of bee stings.

Sometimes you give me no treble clef
Letting me run wild on that long line
With no fuel left
To give that world shine.

Your confidence is transferred
To my dark and rigid silhouette
Giving life to the long deferred
Hidden and vibrant lad-ette.

You leave me in and out
Every now and then
But I'll never be in doubt
Of giving rhythm to that fountain pen

Your inked-up animation
On that flat white paper
Forms a solid foundation
For the expression of this vocal vapour.

Always, I treasure your presence
Your firm and solid place in my heart
Allows me, to understand the silly sense
Of all that transpires, in this art.

To release the pain
Is spiritual gain

Through expression of words
Relaxed are the nerves

NORTHERN HEALING

The golden days, followed by the
Sunset haze, help the healing of all
Those stuck within the maze. Those
Left and right turns seem never ending.
Of all those suffering, we are bound
Together, yet know not one another. We are
'A phone call away,' but we are lost astray. In this
Wicked wilderness, of all that hinders us.
A step onto that dessert sand
Makes us feel so grand, with nothing
Being in sight for a few hours of flight.
At the edge of reality, my eyes see destiny.

A life, now, of peace and release.
A new un-buttoned culture lets me
Unravel into nature, letting me finally
Explore all the open and closed doors.
In mind's sight: the yellow water billabong,
Where paradise is now not far along.
Renewing soul and freshening mind.
Erasing that button of rewind. Where,
Past memories and anecdotes

Get dropped and dissolved along
The gravel road while playing this song,
Of good old dreamtime and tune
Of tranquil, left on streaming.

As my time expires, the land
Requires that I now retire and return,
but in conflict
I yearn to remain standing on,
This boab tree plane.
A dozen moments here is not enough.
It is very rough and with a puff,
I just say, it is tough.
To return back to perdition, where I
Will merge with old and lost tradition.
Like the goo built up in traditional stew,
It has no place,
No longer serves, and is not what
I deserve. As I swerve and curve,
I hold the ground, all bound
And so drowned in the red sand
Where I confidently stand

Hand in hand, so strong
And chain so long – like a necklace
Wrapped around my neck in embrace.

I make a note to return,
So stern in my decision with an extreme
Regime of precision.

The power of the land
Permits me to strongly stand
And balance the tight rope
Walking across, finding hope

FORWARD

In the lake
I must create a ripple.
No wings or paddles.
It is impossible.
How do I create waves –
With no resistance?
For the energy to move
Like a bird in the wind
Or wind through pipe.

I must create an effect
With no medium to strike.

Will it be a bridge?
That will help hinge
The void between
Stillness and activity,
The hammer and screw
Ready to build
But no builder in sight.

No wetness without dry
No rain without sun

And no fall without height
So the only way through

This stagnant stillness
Is through movement,
For then I shall reach turf
That cuddles me tight
In this hurricane of thought
And then storm in drought.

The moon in motion
Melts the ice, so frozen
Stimulating inner emotion –
Up and down, rises the ocean.
The tide will then embrace me
Taking me to point B
Where I will foresee
The visions that wait
To be heroic in action

With initial traction
To step ahead
And not be stuck in bed.

It is through stagnation
That one creates motion
After sitting so still
With nothing to fulfil
An idea will be planted,
Which will begin to create
A footprint in front
Acting as the construct
For a new path in sight
En' route to white light

In Close

Everything in the 'now' will be okay
Never again to be lost (astray)
In the wilderness of the blaze
And depression in the maze.

Now, in my hand, the compass
Of staying whole and in oneness,
Pointing north, is to my heart
Where I aim to throw that dart.

•••

"Everything will be okay"

END

•••○••

AUTHOR BIO

Natalie Neckovska is a poet, blog writer and author of her debut poetry collection, Shadow Paradise.

Born and raised in Sydney, Australia, Natalie has pursued her literary journey in the last decade, while working casually in other fields of work. Initially, volunteering her time to write for a bridal content company, producing articles and content for both magazine and website platforms, eventually branching off to create her own blog website, as a foundation for her career in writing.

The inspiration for Shadow Paradise was birthed through Natalie's passion for producing captivating poetry. Coupled with this, her experience with drug addiction, withdrawal and depression, acted as the framework for Shadow Paradise. Natalie wanted to share awareness and knowledge on how these experiences are commonplace in society and often go unmissed. Through Shadow Paradise, light is shed upon these societal issues, through offering hope, healing and finding inner freedom.

Through continually creating poetry, Natalie's passion is to continue to publish her work and share her art.

Lightning Source UK Ltd.
Milton Keynes UK
UKHW010712020822
406728UK00002B/457